THE DI

AND

SISTER FAUSTINA

by
Fr. Andrew Witko

*All booklets are published thanks to the
generous support of the members of the
Catholic Truth Society*

CATHOLIC TRUTH SOCIETY
PUBLISHERS TO THE HOLY SEE

CONTENTS

INTRODUCTION

"He who trusts in My mercy will not perish." This extraordinary promise of the Saviour, the essence of the devotion to the Divine Mercy which Pope John Paul II called "the best antibiotic for the illnesses of the contemporary world", in his conversation with Cardinal Andrzej Maria Deskur, was conveyed to us by the Apostle of the Divine Mercy - Sister Faustina Kowalska, a Polish nun from the Congregation of Our Lady of Mercy. Our Lord chose this simple, uneducated woman to remind the world of the forgotten truth about the Divine Mercy, and to give new forms of the devotion to the Divine Mercy. This Sister, so modest and unpretentious during her life, is now perceived as one of the great mystics of the Church. She astonishes us by her deep understanding of the articles of faith, while teaching us to trust in the Divine Mercy and love our neighbour. This text has been prepared, to meet the demand for information about the life and mission of the Apostle of the Divine Mercy, both for those who have some knowledge about the Polish Mystic, and those who have not heard about the devotion to the Divine Mercy.

In the first part, the life of Sister Faustina will be presented, based mainly on the sworn testimonies of witnesses in the Informative Process, whose documents, published in Latin in 1984 by *Congregatio de Causis Sanctorum* have not as yet been fully used in the numerous biographies about the life of Sister Faustina. In the second part, we will try to show the devotion to the Divine Mercy in the forms described by Sister Faustina, and will discuss the various ways in which this Devotion may be practised and the extraordinary promises attached to it.

We wish to express our gratitude to everyone, who contributed to the publishing of this work: to Ms Anna Kucala from Cracow for helping to prepare the text, to Ms Vera Barber from Eastbourne, and Fr Anton Guziel from Birmingham for providing valuable comments, and to the CTS Publishing House for bringing it to the readers.

THE APOSTLE OF THE DIVINE MERCY
SISTER FAUSTINA

Faustina's family life

Helena Kowalska - later Sister Faustina - was born on 25th August, 1905 in the village of Glogowiec close to Leczyca in Central Poland, the third of ten children in the poor peasant family of Stanislaw Kowalski (who died in 1946) and Marianna née Babel (who died in 1965). Two days after her birth, she was baptised at St Casimir's the parish church of Świnice Warckie by the parish priest the Rev Józef Chodyński. The children were brought up mainly by the mother. Their father, besides working on his small farm, also worked as a carpenter to keep his large family. However, in spite of poverty, and hard work, there was a very pious Christian atmosphere in their home. The children were brought up in discipline and obedience, and great stress was put on their religious life. At the same time, they were getting used to work - from small household duties to hard labour on the farm.

When Helena was seven, she heard God's voice in her soul for the first time, calling her to a more perfect life. This voice was to grow stronger and stronger as the years passed, urging her to fulfil her mission in the Congregation chosen for her by God.

In 1914, at the age of nine, Helena received Holy Communion for the first time. It was a source of great joy for her, which she wanted to share with everybody. On her way home from church afterwards, she did not accompany other girls but proceeded alone. Asked by a neighbour why she was walking all by herself, she answered: "The Lord Jesus is accompanying me." From that day, Helena changed a great deal. "She always wanted to go to church, her mother recalled, she avoided company, and wanted to be left alone."

Their church was about two kilometres away, but because of housework, Helena was not often allowed to go there. Sunday mass was very important to her, she never wanted to miss it. But sometimes she was not able to attend, since there was only one mass in her parish church, and somebody had to stay at home to keep an eye on the household and the younger children. Besides, not all the children possessed so-called 'Sunday clothes' so they had to share. Another obstacle was the need to keep watch on the grazing cattle. This order was very strict. One day when it was Helena's turn to do it, she got up quietly, very early while it was still dark, left home through a window, and took the cattle out to pasture. Later in the morning, her father was shocked to find the cow-shed wide open and the cattle missing. But before he had time to do anything, Helena came back with the cows, singing happily, because now, having done her duty, she could go to church. Helena's way of leaving the house through a window, became a habit and nobody was surprised any more to see the cow-shed door open very early in the morning.

Compassion for the poor

From a very early age Helena was very sensitive to poverty. When she was ten, she dressed as a beggar, and went from house to house in her village, asking for alms. When she came back home she said: "It is terrible to be poor. How much they have to suffer and bear in order to feed themselves." She gave everything she had been given to the poor.

Two years later, she organised a raffle for the poor. She asked the neighbours for small objects to be offered as prizes, and made and sold lottery tickets. All the money, thus earned, she took to the parish priest, and asked him to give it to the needy.

In September 1917, Helena started her primary education in a school in Swinice Warckie. Although her education was very short - it lasted for only three years - Helena was a very diligent and reliable student. Her favourite subject was religion, and she got the best marks in it. On one occasion two girls did not want to sit with Helena, at the same desk, because she was poorly dressed. When Helena started crying, her teacher tried to console her: "It does not matter that you are poorly dressed - you are a better student." And indeed, Helena was a good student and an avid reader, although she did not have much free time. She often read books while tending the cows and then shared with her friends what she had learnt. She used to tell other children about the lives of the Saints which she knew from her own reading or from listening to her father reading aloud in the evenings.

Helena loved praying, and singing religious songs. Sometimes she did this at night. She often told her family about a dream in which she saw the Mother of God in a beautiful garden, adding: "Wait and see, I will not stay with you, I will leave home." Her brothers and sisters laughed at her, but she maintained that she would join 'the pilgrims'. She used the word 'pilgrim' which she remembered from her father's reading in the evenings, because she did not know anything about religious orders, at that time.

When her parents did not let her attend mass on Sunday, she took a prayer book, withdrew from their sight, and prayed piously. Her mother was sometimes angry with her, but Helena did not stop until she had finished all the prayers for that day. Then she came to her mother and said: "Mummy, do not be angry, because Jesus would be more angry if I did not do that."

Sometimes on Sunday, Helena was allowed to play with friends. She agreed with joy, and went to the garden where, on a pear tree, there was an image of Our Lady which had been made by her father. She dressed the image with flowers and prayed with joy. In May, she prepared seats for the family members, who gathered there to sing the litany and songs to Our Lady. In her room, she also had Mary's statue, which she took care of and adorned with flowers.

Although the Kowalskis were poor, Helena was not interested in worldly possessions. She was the only one in the family who did not care about clothes at all; she never asked her mother to buy her anything, but willingly wore her older sisters' dresses which, although old, were clean and looked neat.

Faustina's vocation

In order to help her parents, Helena left home at the age of sixteen, and went into service with the Bryszewski family, bakers in Aleksandrów. When, after a year, she came back and told her parents about her wish to enter a convent, they strongly opposed this move explaining that they could not give her a dowry. She replied: "The Lord Jesus will accept me without any money." After a few days at home, she went to Łódź to look for a new job. She started working for three tertiaries of St Francis - while accepting this job she made sure she would be able to attend mass every day, as well as to visit the sick and the dying.

From February 1923, she worked for Marcjanna Sadowska for more than a year, showing great faith and zeal. "She was always fasting," testified Sadowska, "all the year on Wednesdays, Fridays and Saturdays, and every day during Lent. On Ash Wednesday she did not even touch food. But she was very good-natured and laughed a lot."

Because she was trying to obey her parents Helena stopped thinking about her vocation, but Christ had His own plans regarding her. Like the apostles who left their fishing and followed Jesus, Helena also experienced a meeting with the Lord. While attending a party with one of her sisters, she saw the suffering Christ at her side, stripped of clothes and covered with wounds. He addressed her saying: "How long shall I put up with you, and how long will you keep putting Me off?" At that moment, the music stopped for her, the company vanished, she slipped out unnoticed, and made her way to the Cathedral of St Stanislaus Kostka. Paying no attention to the few people present, she fell prostrate before the Blessed Sacrament, and begged the Lord to let her know His will. It was then that she heard these words in her soul: "Go at once to Warsaw; you will enter a convent there."

So she packed her things, took them to her uncle Rapacki and left them there to be given to her sisters. She took only one dress with her. Her uncle saw her off to the railway station. Both of them cried, but Helena did not hesitate - she left her old life behind and went forth to experience her great adventure with Jesus.

Looking for a convent

When she arrived in Warsaw, she went to the Rev Jakub
Dabrowski, the parish priest of St James' parish church in
Ochota, and asked him to help her to enter a convent. He
sent her to his friends - the Lipszyc family in Ostrówek
near Klembów. She stayed with them, and went to
Warsaw in search of a convent that would accept her. But
she was refused everywhere. The main reason was the
fact that Helena did not have a dowry which was very
important at that time.

Finally, Helena knocked at the door of the
Congregation of the Sisters of Our Lady of Mercy at 3/9
Żytnia Street in Warsaw. She was received by Sister
Malgorzata Gimbutt who spoke with her for a short
time, and then described her to Mother General
Leonarda Cielecka as 'no one special, thin, weak and
poor.' The superior of the Warsaw house, Mother
General to be, Sister Michaela Moraczewska, who
overheard these words, decided to see the candidate for
herself. Mother Leonarda agreed and she went
downstairs. She saw the candidate through the open
door and she also decided that she was 'no one special.'
She was on the point of dismissing the candidate, when
it occurred to her to have a word with her. After a short
conversation, she decided that Helena was sensible,
sincere, modest and had a nice face and smile. So she
told Helena to go to the Lord of the house and ask him

if He would accept her. Helena understood at once that she was to ask Jesus. She went to the chapel and asked: "Lord of this house, do You accept me?" She heard the words: "I do accept you; you are in My Heart."

Working for a dowry

Although Sister Michaela liked Helena, she wanted to get more information about her. So she advised Helena to work as a domestic with the people with whom she was staying and earn enough money for a small dowry, needed to enter the convent. Helena obeyed, went back to Aldona Lipszycowa and worked there for a year. She took all the money she had saved for her dowry to Żytnia Street.

Later Aldona Lipszycowa described Helena as a very reliable worker, joyful, full of spirit and with a sense of humour. She was treated as a member of the family, not as a servant. Helena's main task was to take care of the children, who simply adored her. She played with them, sang songs, was always cheerful and never became angry. She also used to sing religious songs, one in particular called: 'Hidden Jesus'.

Although Mrs Lipszycowa was very pious, she did not understand Helena's vocation. That was why she tried to make other plans for her worker's future life. Helena's reaction to this was to make a vow of perpetual chastity, at vespers, during the octave of Corpus Christi in 1925.

FAUSTINA ENTERS THE SISTERS OF OUR LADY OF MERCY

At last on 1st August 1925, Helena applied again to the Congregation of the Sisters of Our Lady of Mercy in Warsaw, and this time she was accepted. She wrote in her Diary: "I felt immensely happy; it seemed to me that I had stepped into the life of Paradise. A single prayer was bursting forth from my heart, one of thanksgiving." However, after only three weeks in the convent, Helena felt a strong temptation to leave the Congregation, and enter a stricter order where there would be more time for prayer. When she was about to do this, she had a vision of Jesus Christ's wounded, bleeding face and heard His words: "It is you who will cause Me this pain if you leave this convent. It is to this place that I called you and nowhere else; and I have prepared many graces for you."

Soon afterwards, Helena fell ill, and her superior sent her to a vacation house of the Congregation in Skolimów to regain her strength. After a short rest there, she came back to Warsaw, and started her postulancy period. At that time she was helping in the kitchen. On one occasion Sister Marcjanna ordered her to wash up after dinner. But Helena was so busily engaged by the other sisters that she did not do it promptly. After 45 minutes, Sister Marcjanna saw the dirty dishes. She told Helena to sit on the table, and started the washing up herself. Sisters passing through the kitchen were surprised, and made some unpleasant comments. Helena was silent, not willing to make any excuses. It was only when one of the sisters ordered her to apologise to Sister Marcjanna that she said how sorry she was. After a few months in Warsaw, at the beginning of January 1926, Helena was sent to complete her postulancy period, and to enter the novitiate in Cracow. Sister Janina Bartkiewicz, who was responsible for the candidates' spiritual life, described Helena as "a soul very closely united with Jesus."

The novitiate

In Cracow, Helena completed her postulancy period under the supervision of Sister Malgorzata Gimbutt and after an eight-day retreat received the veil. Deeply moved by this, she fainted twice during the ceremony - in the chapel, when she was to receive the habit and later when she was putting it on. She wrote in *The Diary* that God let her know then, how much she was to suffer during her life. What she had experienced was only 'a moment of that suffering.' Afterwards, her soul was filled with overwhelming joy ... The outward symbol of changing into a new person was also a change of name - from that moment, Helena bore the name of Sister Maria Faustina.

The ceremony was the beginning of the two-year novitiate, a new stage in the development of the spiritual

life. According to the other sisters, Sister Faustina was
the first one to mortify herself by wearing a hair shirt,
spiked bracelets and chains, or practising self-flagellation.
Her first duties were in the kitchen, where she worked
with great zeal and diligence. As she confessed later, the
most difficult task for her was to kill fish. But on the
other hand, she was very brave and outspoken in religious
matters. One day, having overheard three older nuns
expressing adverse criticism of their confessors, Sister
Faustina addressed them with the following words:
"Excuse me, but Jesus does not like it, so stop this
conversation."

In June, 1926, there was an administrative change in
the novitiate - Sister Józefa Brzoza was appointed as
the Directress of Novices in place of Malgorzata
Gimbutt. She was young, but very experienced in the
problems of the spiritual life. She was to play a major
role in the spiritual development of Sister Faustina.
When, at the end of the first year of the novitiate, Sister
Faustina was experiencing a period of spiritual
darkness and misery, her directress encouraged her to
trust in God and be faithful to Him. On Good Friday,
16th April 1928, during the evening adoration, the
flame of Divine Love encompassed the heart of the
suffering novice. Jesus let her know how much He had
suffered for her, so that she would realise that her
sufferings were nothing compared to His love.

Temporary vows

A few days later, on 30th April 1928, Sister Faustina took
her first temporary vows. Her parents also attended this
ceremony. Her father asked Faustina how she felt in the
convent and if she liked being a nun. She replied:
"Daddy, I am so happy. Why should I complain if I live
with the Lord Jesus under one roof. I pledged myself to
Him, so He is my husband and your son-in-law." Her
father cried when he heard this; and he also cried, when
he told this to his relatives and friends.

After the first profession of temporary vows Sister
Faustina started on her monastic way of life, which led
her through the many houses of the Congregation - the
Generalate in Żytnia Street in Warsaw, Vilnius, Grochów
in Warsaw, Żytnia again and Kiekrz near Poznań. She
worked mainly as a cook. During her short stay in Kiekrz,
on a one-day retreat, she stopped on the shore of the lake
contemplating her surroundings. Suddenly she saw Jesus,
who said to her: "All this I created for you, My spouse;
and know that all this beauty is nothing, compared to
what I have prepared for you in eternity."

In the middle of 1930, Sister Faustina was sent to the
house of the Congregation in Plock where she worked
by turns in the bakery, the kitchen and the baker's shop.
She also stayed in the house of the Congregation in
Biala, ten kilometres from the convent in Plock. One
weekday because there had been a severe frost, and a

heavy snowfall the superior decided that the sisters would not be able to attend mass in the church, one kilometre away. Hearing that, Sister Faustina asked: 'Perhaps I could get permission to go to church?' The superior agreed on condition that Faustina would wear a huge sheepskin coat, used only for travelling. However, Sister Faustina did not hesitate, put on the coat and went to church. The parish priest could not hide his astonishment when he saw a nun in a huge sheepskin coat, stepping out to receive Holy Communion.

Sister Faustina's visions begin

When Faustina came back to Plock she had a vision that was to play a crucial role in her life and mission; and, to some extent, in the life of the whole world. In the evening of the 22nd February 1931, when she was in her cell she saw 'the Lord Jesus clothed in a white garment. One hand [was] raised in the gesture of blessing, the other was touching the garment at the breast. From beneath the garment, slightly drawn aside at the breast, there were emanating two large rays, one red, the other pale.' Then she heard Jesus' words: "Paint an image according to the pattern you see, with the signature: Jesus, I trust in You. I desire that this image be venerated, first in your chapel, and [then] throughout the world. I promise that the soul that will venerate this image will not perish."

When Sister Faustina told her confessor what had happened, he did not understand and explained that Jesus wanted her to paint His image in her soul. But when she left the confessional she heard the following words: "My image is already in your soul. I desire that there [should] be a Feast of Mercy. I want this image, which you will paint with a brush, to be solemnly blessed on the first Sunday after Easter; that Sunday is to be the Feast of Mercy."

Sister Faustina turned to her superior, Sister Róża Klobukowska, for help. But her superior did not take her seriously and said, "All right, paint." Sister Faustina tried to sketch the image in crayon on the wall, but in vain. Meanwhile, the town children kept stopping in front of the Congregation's house in the evenings, to watch rays coming out of one of the windows. It was Sister Faustina's window. Angry nuns asked their superior what Sister Faustina was doing that caused the children to stop in the street to watch the rays coming out of her window? Sister Róża gave a non-committal reply: "How do I know?"

Searching for a painter

At the beginning of 1932, Sister Faustina offering paints and a paintbrush, asked Sister Bożena, secretly, to paint an image of Jesus Christ adding that she could not paint it herself. Sister Bożena could not paint either, so she was unable to help. In order to make her friend happy, she wanted to give Sister Faustina a picture of Jesus.

The atmosphere in the Plock convent was becoming less and less favourable towards Sister Faustina. Some sisters treated her with reserve, often saying unkind things to her. But the time for taking her perpetual vows was approaching. According to the constitution of the Congregation, after taking temporary vows five times, nuns are obliged to spend a period of *third probation* lasting five months. Therefore in November 1932, Sister Faustina left Plock and went to Walendów, stopping on her way in Warsaw, to make a retreat and to begin the next stage of her religious life.

On 1st December 1932, she began the *third probation* under the supervision of Sister Malgorzata Gimbutt. During that time, she worked in the vestry, or clothes storeroom. Having direct access to Mother General, she approached her, with Jesus' request, to paint a picture with the signature *Jesus, I trust in You.* Sister Michaela Moraczewska, Superior General since 1928, the one who received Faustina into the convent back in 1924, already knew about the problem from Róża Klobukowska. But she also treated Faustina's request with scepticism.

After the *third probation*, Sister Faustina left for Cracow to make a retreat, before her profession of perpetual vows, which took place on 1st May 1933, in Lagiewniki, Cracow. From that time, her unity with Christ was closer and more intimate. Mother General intended to keep Sister Faustina in Cracow afterwards, so that she would have a good confessor in the person of the Rev Józef Andrasz SJ. However, when a request for a gardener arrived from Vilnius, she decided to send Sister Faustina there. The latter knew almost nothing about gardening, but that is how God's designs concerning her mission of the Divine Mercy were to be fulfilled.

Sister Faustina moves to Vilnius

In May 1933, Sister Faustina left Cracow for Vilnius. On her way there, she stopped in Czestochowa to visit the shrine of the Black Madonna. Looking at the holy image, she became so engrossed in prayer, that the superior of the house had to send for her so that she would not miss her train. When she arrived in Vilnius, it appeared that Jesus had prepared a great surprise for His servant. During confession, she met a priest whom she had previously seen twice in her visions, and who was to become her spiritual adviser and help her in her mission. His name was Michal Sopoćko, who was confessor to the Congregation of the Sisters of Our Lady of Mercy as well as theology professor at the Stefan Batory University in Vilnius. During confession, Sister Faustina bared her soul to him and told him about Jesus' orders. At first the priest treated these revelations with extreme caution. When Faustina insisted, during her subsequent confessions, he considered giving up his post as the Congregation's confessor. However, it never came to that. To make sure that Sister Faustina was not mentally ill, he sent her to psychiatrists and gathered information about her from her superiors. The results of the examination carried out by Doctor Helena Maciejewska and the opinion of the Vilnius superior, Sister Irena Krżyzanowska, and the Mother General Michaela Moraczewska were so favourable that the Rev Sopoćko changed his attitude towards Sister Faustina. He decided to help her to have the image of the Divine Mercy painted - more out of curiosity, and not because he was completely convinced of the supernatural nature of Faustina's visions.

Kazimirowski paints the first Divine Mercy Image

A Vilnius artist, Eugeniusz Kazimirowski, was chosen to paint the image. He was an average painter and was chosen for practical reasons - he lived in the same house as Rev Sopoćko. Thus, from 2nd January 1934, Sister Faustina went regularly, with her superior - Sister Irena and later Sister Borgia Tichy - to Holy Mass at *Ostra Brama* every Saturday, *Ostra Brama* was the most important Shrine of Our Lady, beside Czestochowa, in pre-war Poland. Our Lady is depicted without the Child, in the aureole of the sun and is known by the name of 'Mother of Mercy.'

They then went on to Rossa, where Father Sopoćko and the artist lived. The superior stayed in the priest's flat, while Sister Faustina instructed the painter in his flat. However, the painting was not as beautiful as Faustina desired. Disappointed with the effect after one of her visits, she went to the chapel and cried bitterly saying: "Who will paint You as beautiful as You are?" It was then that she heard a voice: "Not in the beauty of the colour, nor of the brush lies the greatness of this image, but in My grace."

After six months the painting was finished. Father Sopoćk paid the artist, took the picture to his flat and later hung it in a dark corridor of the Bernardine Sisters' convent near St Michael's Church, where he was the rector. Sister Faustina was deeply disappointed that the image, which was to be honoured all over the world, was hidden within the convent enclosure so that nobody could see it.

The image of the Divine Mercy shows Jesus wearing a white robe. His eyes are looking slightly downwards, and His right hand is raised to the shoulder level in the gesture of blessing. His left hand, meanwhile, is touching the garment at the breast where two large rays come out - one red, the other pale. Jesus himself explained the meaning of these rays: "The two rays denote Blood and Water. The pale ray stands for the Water which makes souls righteous. The red ray stands for the Blood which is the life of souls." One of the essential parts of the image is the signature inscribed on the frame with the words *Jesus, I trust in You*.

The diary

Sister Faustina's confessions were so long that they took up a lot of the confessor's time and made the other sisters

**The first picture of the Divine Mercy,
painted by Eugeniusz Kazimirowski 1934, Vilnius.**

upset. Therefore, Father Sopoćko asked her to confess only her sins and to write down everything else she considered important, in a notebook so that he could have a look at it from time to time. This is the origin of her *Diary*. After a few months, when Rev Sopoćko went to the Holy Land for a few weeks, she burnt it, persuaded to do so by an imaginary angel. The priest made her rewrite the destroyed part from memory as a penance, and write down her current experiences simultaneously. Because of this, *The Diary* lacks chronological order.

On 29th March 1934 (Maundy Thursday), Sister Faustina made a voluntary offering of herself for the conversion of sinners, particularly those who had lost hope in the Divine Mercy. With total subjection to God's will, she expressed readiness to accept all the suffering, fears and terrors with which sinners are filled. In return, she was ready to give them all the consolations which her soul received from communion with God.

Gardener at Vilnius

In Vilnius Sister Faustina was gardener. Although she knew little about gardening, she worked hard and improved her skills; and got wonderful results. On one occasion when Sister Felicja, noticing Faustina's problems at work, asked her how she was doing, she replied: "I like it wherever God's will puts me." Obedience to her superiors and the love that she put into her work made it possible for her to obtain results that others could not get. On another occasion when the Mother General was showing some important guests around the convent, one of them exclaimed: "You must have a real expert gardener here."

By means of gardening, and through the fruits of her work, she wanted to give joy to Jesus and to mankind. She always took the most beautiful flowers she had grown, to decorate the altar. The sisters were favourably impressed to see her offering flowers to the Lord. Sister Fabiana remembered that one day Faustina brought a white primrose in bloom, put it in front of the Christmas crib and left. The plant fell from the height of 1.5 metres but it remained intact. Another sister recalled that Faustina's greatest pleasure was to give the first fruits of the season to Mother Superior and the chaplain.

In the evening of 26th October, 1934, while coming into to supper from the garden, with some of the girls, Sister Faustina saw the Lord Jesus above the chapel looking just as she saw Him long ago in Plock. The two rays emanating from His Heart covered the chapel, the infirmary and spread out over the whole city and the world. One of the girls also saw this unusual phenomenon - the two rays - but she did not see Jesus.

On 15th February 1935, Sister Faustina received a letter from her family with sad news - her mother was seriously ill and wanted to see her beloved child before she died. Having obtained permission from her superior,

Faustina left for home immediately and arrived at Glogowiec on the next day. Her dying mother felt better, the moment she saw her daughter. According to her sister Józefa, Faustina told her mother that she had a long life before her but that her father, although in better health, would die earlier. After a few days with her family, having spoken to many relatives and neighbours, who paid numerous visits to Sister Faustina during her stay at home, she returned to Vilnius to her duties.

In April 1935, Sister Faustina told Father Sopoćko that Jesus wished the image of the Divine Mercy to be displayed for public veneration in *Ostra Brama* at the conclusion of the Jubilee Year of the Redemption of the World. He could grant that wish because he was invited to the celebration as a preacher. He accepted the invitation on one condition - that the image would be placed in *Ostra Brama*.

Celebrations concluding the Jubilee Year of the Redemption of the World took place on 26th-28th April 1935, and the image of the Divine Mercy was transferred to *Ostra Brama* and placed in a high window. Sister Faustina decorated it with green wreaths. It could be seen from far away and made a great impression on the participants. They considered it to be a version of the image of the Sacred Heart although they were surprised that the heart itself was not depicted. In his sermon on the first day, Father Sopoćko talked about the Divine Mercy. Pointing to the picture, painted by Eugeniusz

Kazimirowski, he said that the Divine Mercy should be worshipped in public. While listening to this sermon, Sister Faustina saw the image come alive, and the rays pierce the hearts of the people gathered there, but not all to the same degree. After the celebrations, the picture was taken back to the cloisters of St Michael's Church and, incredibly enough, hung with the image facing the wall, so that nobody could see it.

The Chaplet of the Divine Mercy

On the 13th and 14th September 1935, Jesus dictated the Chaplet of the Divine Mercy to Sister Faustina. He called it a prayer 'to appease His wrath.' He promised many graces to everybody reciting it, i.e. the grace of conversion and a holy death in the state of grace: "Whoever will recite it, will receive great mercy at the hour of death. Priests will recommend it to sinners as their last hope of salvation. Even if there were a sinner most hardened, if he were to recite this chaplet only once, he would receive grace from My infinite mercy."

From the middle of 1935, Sister Faustina often heard Jesus' order to found a new community whose task would be to spread the devotion to the Divine Mercy. According to her, this congregation would have three stages. The first one would consist of sisters living in enclosure and who would beg for the Divine Mercy for the whole world; the second would be formed by an active congregation, whereas the third one would be a great apostolic movement consisting mainly of laity. In conversation with Father Sopoćko, Faustina also mentioned a congregation of brothers of a similar character. She confided these revelations to Michaela Moraczewska, her Mother General who demanded to see a definite sign and hesitated for a long time thus causing a lot of suffering to poor Faustina who was just then diagnosed with tuberculosis. Her wish to leave the congregation in order to found a new one, prompted the Superior General to transfer Sister Faustina from Vilnius.

On 25th March 1936, Sister Faustina came to Walendów near Warsaw where she received a warm welcome from the sisters. It was there that she met Sister Beata, who was to stay in Walendów for only a month. One day Sister Faustina told her to be prepared for a longer stay there: "I will be here for only a short time," she said, "while you will stay for a few years." Sister Beata did not welcome these words, as she hoped to leave the place as soon as possible. When Sister Faustina was transferred to Derdy and later to Cracow, while she stayed in Walendów for eleven years, she wondered how Sister Faustina could have known that? Had her superiors told her?

Sister Faustina goes to Cracow

After a short stay in Derdy, on 11th May 1936, Sister Faustina left for a permanent stay in Cracow. It was there that she was to live the last months of her short life. At first, she worked in the garden. She gathered unusually large crops, much bigger than the other sisters. Sister Klemensa testified that the cucumbers were so plentiful that full baskets of them were gathered daily. The same happened with strawberries - 150 kilograms were picked, daily, from a small plot of land. Also tomatoes grew in great numbers - some plants bore 80 of them.

Hard work in the garden did not weaken Sister Faustina's communion with Jesus. On the contrary, she often prayed with the girls while working, and when she was free - especially on Sundays - she spent long hours in the chapel. Nothing could disturb her then. One of the choir members recalled the old wooden stairs which made a terrible noise when they climbed them. The sisters always scolded them and told them to be quiet, whereas Sister Faustina, whose kneeler was closest to the stairs, never paid any attention. "She always knelt immersed in prayer, as if the world did not exist."

When her work made longer prayer impossible, she tried to visit the chapel more often. For just a few minutes she knelt down before the Blessed Sacrament, 'sometimes just smiled and went out to work,' to continue doing her duties with renewed energy. There was no affectation or artificiality in her behaviour, 'she was extraordinarily ordinary' - as one of her superiors described her. Some sisters were annoyed at seeing a radiant smile always on her face when she received Holy Communion, which was a sign of her union with God. Love for God made her contemplate the Way of the Cross daily, adore the Blessed Sacrament, and do all the obligatory spiritual exercises dutifully. With her superiors' permission, she often lay prostrate in the chapel after 9 pm when there were no sisters present. "There was something elusive about her, something that emanated from her personality which some sisters could feel occasionally and even sometimes be irritated by it," said Sister Borgia, her superior. The fact that she was different, made the other sisters assume an unkind attitude towards Sister Faustina; trying to tease her they called her bigot, or princess. Faustina usually did not react to such names; only once she said: "True, I am a princess, because the royal blood of Christ is in my veins."

Daily her health deteriorated. On 9th December 1936, her superiors sent her to the hospital in Pradnik near Cracow, a sanatorium for tuberculosis patients. After her arrival there she was soon well liked both by medical staff and other patients. Everybody was surprised that she was always smiling in spite of her pain, and her unusual missionary zeal amazed even the priests. Once she confessed to Sister Serafina that "the patients are left alone because the priest leaves for the town early; but fortunately, I can usually be with the dying which makes me very happy." She prepared many dying patients for confession and Holy Communion and kept them company praying for a peaceful death. However, when her superior forbade these practices for her health's sake she obeyed immediately. With the doctor's permission, she was allowed to spend Christmas in the convent, but later returned to hospital, where she stayed until 27th March 1937.

Permission to found a new congregation

In May 1937, the Mother General, having consulted the general council, granted Sister Faustina permission to leave the Congregation of the Sisters of Our Lady of Mercy if, according to God's will she was to found a new order. This decision took Sister Faustina by surprise. She immediately felt lost, lonely, unable to do anything. Father Sopoćko, who was consulted in this matter, replied that both her confessor's and Mother General's permission were not valid if Sister Faustina did not get an explicit order to leave the Congregation. At the end of Faustina's life Father Sopoćko came to the conclusion that Sister Faustina was not able to start a new congregation, in the same way as she was unable to paint the image of the Divine Mercy, by herself.

At the end of July, Sister Faustina went to Rabka for a few days but she felt even worse there and returned to Cracow very soon. Because of her deteriorating health, her job was changed from gardener to gatekeeper. Sisters testified later, that Faustina was very gentle and kind as a gatekeeper - particularly to the poor, who often came to the convent begging for food or alms. There were many of them, but Faustina never refused to go to the kitchen to ask for something to eat although this made the cooks angry with her.

One rainy day, a poor young man, in rags and very cold, came to the gate and asked for something to eat. Sister Faustina went to the kitchen, found some soup, put some bread crumbs into it and offered it to the beggar. As she was taking the bowl from him, she recognised Jesus, but He vanished from her sight.

When Sister Damiana visited her in the autumn, Faustina said to her: "I am feeling really bad but I hope that Jesus will not surprise me because I am to die at the age of thirty-three." However, her illness was progressing fast, and she had to stay in hospital longer and longer. Some sisters suspected her of simulating her illness, and accused her of excessive preoccupation with her own health.

Observation of the hour of Christ's Death

In October 1937, Jesus instructed Sister Faustina to observe the hour of His death: "At three o'clock, implore My mercy, especially for sinners; and, if only for a brief moment, immerse yourself in My Passion, particularly in My abandonment at the moment of agony. This is the hour of great mercy for the whole world. I will allow you to enter into My mortal sorrow. In this hour, I will refuse nothing to the soul that makes a request of Me in virtue of My

Passion..." The instruction to observe the hour of Jesus' death was the fourth task given to Sister Faustina regarding forms of devotion to the Divine Mercy. The previous tasks, referring to the image and to the Feast, as well as to the Chaplet of the Divine Mercy were given to Faustina in Plock (the former ones) and in Vilnius (the latter one).

In the spring of 1938, Sister Faustina's health deteriorated so much that she was sent again to the hospital in Pradnik. In the evening of 21st April Sacred Heart Sister Dawida who was taking care of Sister Faustina, told her that she was too weak and ill to receive Holy Communion the following day. In obedience to God's will Faustina did not protest, but in the morning she prepared herself for the Sacrament. When her love and desire had overwhelmed her, at her bedside she saw a Seraph who gave her Holy Communion saying: 'Behold the Lord of Angels.' This was repeated for thirteen days.

When she had recovered a little, she tried to attend mass in the hospital chapel. Seeing her taking great pains to walk, somebody told the hospital director, Doctor Adam Silberg, but he answered: "She is an extraordinary sister, I saw her walk to the chapel holding on to the wall. Nobody else could do that, so I cannot forbid her to go to the chapel." The director always visited Sister Faustina's room at the end of his daily inspection. When some people expressed surprise, he explained to them: A good child is always visited at the very end.

Sister Faustina stopped writing her Diary in June 1938, when it became too difficult for her. In August she wrote her last letter to the Mother General Michaela Moraczewska in which she wrote the following words: "My longing for God is growing every day, I do not fear death, peace reigns in my soul." She thanked the Superior General for everything she had experienced in the Congregation, apologised for her offences and faults and ended her moving letter with the words: "Goodbye, dearest Mother, we shall meet in Heaven, at the foot of God's throne. And now, let the Divine Mercy be glorified by us and through us."

The last months

The crisis came on 24th August 1938. The superior of the Cracow house, Sister Irena spent the night at Sister Faustina's bedside. Seeing that the end was near she suggested that Sister Faustina should receive the Sacrament of the Anointing of the Sick and Faustina agreed. After some time, when she was better again, she told Sister Irena that she had known she would not die then but she had agreed to receive the Sacrament to obey her superior, because the superior's will is God's will.

At the end of August and early September, Father Sopoćko visited Sister Faustina in hospital a few times. She told him then, that the spreading of the devotion to the Divine Mercy would encounter great difficulties and that the

Apostolic See would issue a decree forbidding the Devotion. Parting with him she said: "See you in the future life!"

On 17th September 1938, she was taken from the hospital in Pradnik to Lagiewniki to enable her to end her life at home in the convent. Dr. Silberg, parting with his patient asked Sister Faustina for the image of St Theresa of the Child Jesus which she had with her all the time. She pointed out to him that a picture from a tuberculosis patient might be infected. But the doctor replied, "Saints do not infect others" and hung the picture over his son's bed.

On 22nd September 1938, feeling that her end was approaching, Sister Faustina, as was the custom, asked pardon of the entire Congregation for her faults and failings. After that, she awaited unity with God in eternity with trust and peace. The sisters were impressed with her serenity in spite of her great suffering. When one sister asked her if she was afraid of death, she answered: "No, I do not fear death, I look forward to it." In her last conversations with her superior Sister Irena, she said that Jesus wanted to distinguish her and to make her a saint. She also added that the Congregation would get many graces, thanks to her. At last she handed her Diary to Sister Irena asking her to deliver it to the Mother General. Obeying her last request, Sister Irena did not look into it, but handed it directly to Mother Michaela.

On 26th September 1938, Father Sopoćko came specially to Cracow from Czestochowa to visit Sister

Faustina for the last time. However, she did not want to talk to him. She only whispered: "Sorry, Father, but now I am busy talking to my Heavenly Father. Whatever I wanted to say, I already have." She gave the impression of being 'an unearthly being' on Father Sopoćko. After that, he no longer had any doubt that "what she had written in her Diary about receiving Holy Communion from an Angel was really true."

On 5th October 1938 - the last day of her life - Sister Faustina announced with delight: "The Lord will take me today!" Suffering intensely, she asked for a painkiller but after a while changed her mind in case Jesus wanted her to suffer. Later when Father Andrasz arrived, Sister Faustina made her last confession, and calmly awaited her departure. At 9 pm the chaplain, Rev Teodor Czaputa with the sisters assembled at her bedside said prayers for the dying and then departed. Sister Faustina died at 10.45 pm Sisters Liguoria and Eufemia who were in her cell at the time said that at the moment of her death Sister Faustina "lifted her eyes, smiled a little, then inclined her head and ended her life without any visible pain."

The next day Sister Faustina's body was transferred to the crypt below the chapel where it remained until the funeral. In death, she looked better than in the last months of her illness, although her body was very thin and emaciated. As one sister said, in the convent "the general atmosphere was not that of depression or melancholy; on the contrary there was a feeling of joy resulting from the conviction that Sister Faustina had gone to Jesus."

On 7th October 1938 - the First Friday of the month - after Matins and two funeral masses, the coffin containing Sister Faustina's body was transferred from the chapel to the convent cemetery and buried in the common grave of the nuns. No members of Faustina's family were present at the funeral because they were not informed about her death at her request - she did not want them to bear any costs.

The beginning of the mission

Sister Faustina was almost forgotten for many years. When the Second World War broke out strange news from Vilnius concerning the devotion to the Divine Mercy began to spread. Surprised sisters kept asking the Mother General about the meaning of this. In 1941, while visiting some of the houses, Mother Michaela acquainted the sisters with Faustina's mission. The nuns received the news with surprise, but also with joy saying: "Our Lady of Mercy - Patron Saint of our Congregation instructed us through the late Sister Faustina to remind the poor sinful world about the Divine Mercy." Thus, one of Sister Faustina's prophecies written in her Diary is becoming true: "I feel certain that my mission will not come to an end upon my death, but will begin."

In 1965-1967 the Informative Process relating to the life and virtues of Sister Faustina was conducted. It was during that time that her remains were exhumed and transferred to a tomb in the chapel of the Sisters of Our Lady of Mercy in Lagiewniki, Cracow. In 1968 the Process of Beatification was formally inaugurated in Rome. It was then that the recovery of an American woman, Maureen Cahill Digan was recognised as miraculous and this fact was conducive to the advancing of the Process.

On 18th April 1993 - the Sunday of the Divine Mercy - the Holy Father John Paul II beatified Sister Faustina. Thus was fulfilled the wish of millions of people who had prayed for her beatification for many years. Seven years later, again on the Sunday of the Divine Mercy, 30th April 2000 Sister Faustina was canonised in Rome.

The last photograph of Sister Faustina.

THE DEVOTION TO THE DIVINE MERCY

The main task of Sister Faustina was to remind the world about the truth of the Divine Mercy and to show new forms of worship. The devotion to the Divine Mercy as propagated by Sister Faustina, based on private visions and connected with many promises, was forbidden in the years 1958-1978. It was only in 1978 that the *Notification* of the Congregation for the Doctrine of the Faith allowed its forms, as described by Sister Faustina, to be reinstated. Therefore it should be realised that the Devotion, which is only generally, and not officially acknowledged by the Church, is still at the formation stage. Theological analysis of Sister Faustina's writings published by the Congregation for the Causes of the Saints proved that her mission was wholly compatible with the teaching of the Church. That is why, the devotion to the Divine Mercy is spreading fast with the approval and support of the Church, and worshippers may practise it without any misgivings.

The Essence of the Devotion

A spirit of trust is the very nature of the devotion to the Divine Mercy. It ensures trustful believers, many graces in this world, and eternal happiness in the next. This trust is the Devotion itself. Without trust it is impossible to benefit from the Devotion. According to the vision of February 1938, the graces are drawn from the source of Mercy by means of one vessel only, namely - trust. The more a man trusts, the more he will receive. Nine times Jesus showed trust, as a necessary condition to obtain all the graces connected with the Devotion.

The Devotion consists in the adoration of Mercy. Numerous visions explain that to adore the Divine Mercy means to trust it. Thus, even if other elements are missing, the trust itself is the Devotion.

Trust, being the essence of the Devotion, means assuming an attitude conforming to Jesus' will, and connected to other acts of Devotion. The vision of December 1937, identifies trust with faith. The vision of February 13th, 1938, connects trust with humility, which is necessary to receive graces from God, who refuses them to the proud, but grants them to the humble of heart. And the vision of June 1938, identifies trust with willingness to repent and accept grace. Jesus also wanted this trust to be persistent and unwavering.

Because trust is the essence of the Devotion, external practice of this Devotion will not merit the graces promised by Jesus unless it is based on absolute trust. Even the most spectacular adoration of the image of the Divine Mercy, will not guarantee any graces connected with the image, if it is merely outward show, and lacking in inner trust. The same refers to the Chaplet of Divine

Mercy - if one recites it without trust one cannot expect to receive the graces promised by Jesus.

Since trust is the Devotion, and because the effects of the Devotion depend on trust, therefore, trust is the most important element of the Devotion. It is *the soul of the Devotion*. The very important role of trust constitutes Jesus' encouragement to everybody practising the Devotion. Since trust implies faith, humility, contrition and unwavering hope, all the people practising the Devotion should endeavour to acquire and develop these virtues in their spiritual lives.

Practising Mercy

According to Sister Faustina's visions, Jesus demanded four times, that His followers should practise mercy. He showed us three ways of exercising mercy towards our neighbour: by deed, by word and by prayer. In the vision of 1st October 1937, He added that if a man does not practise mercy during his life, he will not receive Jesus' mercy on the day of Judgement. Therefore, works of mercy are, after trust, the next most important element of the Devotion. However, they are neither indispensable nor essential to the Devotion.

Exercising mercy depends on the kind of the Devotion. In *Positio super scriptis* two kinds of Devotion are distinguished: simple and integral ones. The former is limited to simple acts of Devotion necessary to obtain the graces connected with them. Thus the Feast of Mercy and connected with it the grace of total forgiveness of sins and punishment, after confession and Holy Communion, is considered to be a simple kind of Devotion. Since confession may directly precede Holy Communion, obtaining the grace of *Second Baptism* cannot depend on works of mercy as there is no time or opportunity to do them. The fact that Jesus did not require the practice of additional works of mercy, makes the grace connected with the Feast of Mercy exceptional.

The Chaplet

Another example of simple Devotion is the Chaplet of Mercy recited by a dying person at the hour of death and which has a promise of a holy death in the state of grace, attached to it. Also in this case there is no opportunity to exercise works of mercy so they cannot be a necessary condition to obtain the graces connected with this act of Devotion. It should be noted, however, that the recitation of the chaplet is an act of mercy in itself since, while saying it, we beg mercy not only for ourselves but also for the whole world.

The Devotion is integral if, besides specific acts, it also comprises the attitude of mercy necessary to obtain the promised graces. Active mercy can be realised in three ways: through deeds, words and prayer, as Jesus told us.

Trust and works of mercy

In the vision of 24th October 1936, Jesus showed a new role of the image of the Divine Mercy. According to previous visions the image was the object of worship and a means of obtaining graces; in the light of this vision it is a sign reminding us to perform works of mercy. Thus the honour given to the image alone, without exercising mercy through deeds, words or prayer, is not the act of Devotion required by Jesus, because it does not entail the graces connected with worshipping the image. As we can see, the veneration of the image is a part of an integral Devotion which involves performing works of mercy as well.

In the light of the above reasoning, it should be said, that it is conditionally necessary to practise mercy in the Devotion. Whoever has the opportunity to perform works of mercy, should do so. If he does not, he cannot get the graces connected with the particular forms of the Devotion. Jesus explained that 'spiritual mercy [...] is much more meritorious' and added that everybody practising the Devotion ought to perform at least one act of mercy a day.

Thus, although acts of mercy do not constitute the very essence of the Devotion - contrary to trust - the conditional necessity of their performance makes us practise love of our neighbour. In this way, the Devotion is part of traditional Christian observance which has been carried out for many hundreds of years.

Now we would like to present and analyse the various forms of the devotion to the Divine Mercy. The distinction will be based on special promises generally applicable not only to Sister Faustina, but also to all those who practise the Devotion. Thus the beautiful novena from *The Diary*, the litany to the Divine Mercy, or the prayer *O Blood and Water*, cannot be included among the forms of the devotion to the Divine Mercy.

The Image

The Image of the Divine Mercy plays a double role in the Devotion. The first one was mentioned in the vision of 1934, when Jesus called the image *a vessel* that people could use to obtain graces from the fountain of mercy. In the vision of December 1935, the image was called *a means* used by Jesus to grant many graces to people.

The other role of the image was shown by Jesus on 24th October 1936, when He described the image as a reminder of the demands of His mercy: trustfulness and deeds of mercy. Therefore, the image may be regarded as a visual summary and depiction of the whole Devotion. Although this role is often forgotten, it is of the utmost importance for the Devotion whose essence is trustfulness, whereas deeds of mercy form its basis. Worshipping the image without performing works of mercy at the same time, would have more in common with idolatry than genuine Christianity.

Jesus' speech about the image which "is to be a reminder of the demands of My mercy, because even the strongest faith is of no avail without works" reminds us of the words taken from the Letter of St James: "Take the case, my brothers, of someone who has never done a single good act but claims that he has faith [...]. What good is that?" Jesus wanted us to practise mercy towards our neighbour because He wanted the Devotion to become a Christian way of life so that it would not remain merely superficial. Thus, the image points to the necessity of performing works of mercy on the one hand, and on the other, reminds us to trust in the Divine Mercy, the visible sign of which is the inscription, *Jesus, I trust in You!*

Veneration in public

Jesus wanted the image to be venerated in public. The visions do not specify the forms of worship so this wish may be understood in different ways. It was Jesus' wish for the image to be venerated publicly on the Feast of Mercy celebrated on *Low Sunday* (the first Sunday after Easter).

An image based on a private vision has to be justified by the Divine Revelation in order to enable its worship in the Church. Therefore the pioneers of the devotion to the Divine Mercy had a seemingly difficult task to show the connection between the image and the Gospel. Sister Faustina's visions explain the meaning of the image, but not comprehensively enough.

Interpreting the image in the light of the Gospel

The theological interpretation of the image was given by Father Michal Sopoćko who explained its meaning on the basis of the Bible and the liturgy. He pointed out the connection between the image and the liturgy of *Low Sunday*. On that day the Gospel which is read during Mass is the passage from St John describing Jesus' arrival at the Cenacle after His Resurrection. Jesus showed the apostles His hands and side and said the words usually connected with the institution of the Sacrament of Penance.

Another scene from St John's Gospel comes to mind when we look at the image of the Divine Mercy - Jesus' side pierced with a lance. Blood and Water came forth as the proof of Jesus' death. According to St John, the blood and water that came out of the Saviour's Heart have a symbolic meaning - they stand for fountains of living Water, the source of life promised by Jesus to everyone who believes in Him. (Cf. *Jn* 7:38 and 1 *Jn* 5:4-10).

In the vision of the first half of 1934, Jesus explained the meaning of the rays, using a metaphor, therefore they must be interpreted accordingly. Saying that "these rays shield souls from the wrath of My Father" He confirmed that the value of Redemption through His death protects us from the Divine anger thus reconciling us with God.

The image of the Divine Mercy represents the central mystery of our faith - the *Paschal Mysterium* as it refers to two great events - the Passion illustrated both by the rays of mercy and the wounds on Jesus' body, and secondly, the meeting of Jesus and the apostles in the Cenacle on Resurrection Day.

The image plays a special role in the Devotion. It is the key to understanding other forms of the Devotion, being at the same time their synthesis, since *Low Sunday*, when the image is adored, marks the end of the novena to the Divine Mercy, which starts on Good Friday, and both the Chaplet and the prayer at the hour of Jesus' death refer to the Passion through which the Divine Mercy can be obtained. The reference to the Passion was manifested in many revelations in which the two rays of mercy came out of the side of the crucified Christ.

According to Father Sopoćko, who played a great role in painting the first picture, the image, in order to comply with Faustina's vision should meet the following requirements. Jesus, dressed in white, should be depicted standing; secondly, there should be visible scars on His hands and feet. His right hand should be raised in a gesture of blessing, whereas His left hand should touch His breast, opening the robe slightly at the Heart (invisible in the picture) from which two rays: one red, the other pale should emanate. Jesus' gaze ought to be like His *gaze from the cross* and under the picture there should be an inscription: *Jesus, I trust in You!*

Two visions which took place at three o'clock on Good Friday in 1935 and 1936, when Sister Faustina saw Jesus crucified are of particular importance. In the first vision Jesus said: "I desire that the image be publicly honoured" and then Sister Faustina saw the rays of mercy coming out of Jesus' Heart. The second vision was very similar. It seems that Jesus' words from the first vision do not have to be treated as an instruction to worship the image of the crucified Christ with two rays coming out from His Heart. However, it should be noted that the Saviour's death and its redeeming value, the greatest proof of the Divine Mercy, would be more clearly visible in such a picture. Thus an image of the crucified Christ with two rays emanating from His breast, together with the inscription *Jesus, I trust in You* could be an object of worship and would probably carry the same promises as the one painted under the personal supervision of Sister Faustina.

The rays of mercy

In the vision of 20th June 1935, Jesus called the rays in the image, *the rays of mercy*. Explaining their meaning in another vision, He said that they stand for blood and water which came out, when His side was pierced on the cross. This is confirmed in the Scripture, as has already been mentioned. In order to reflect this, the colour of the rays must be exactly as Sister Faustina described in her *Diary* - red and pale. It is a mistake to depict the latter ray as *white*. Both the visions and the biblical context clearly speak about a pale ray. The Devotion has nothing in common with Polish nationalism. Nothing was ever written by Sister Faustina to make us suppose that the rays stand for the Polish national colours, not even a hint allowing such interpretation can be found in *The Diary*.

St. Thomas Aquinas in *Summa theologica* associated Blood and Water, symbolised by the rays, with the Sacrament of Baptism and the Eucharist: "Sacraments of the Church get power from Christ's suffering - it is this power that is joined with us [and acts in us] when we receive the Sacraments. As a sign of this - Blood and Water came out from Jesus' side on the cross; one of them stands for Baptism, the other for the Eucharist: the two most important Sacraments."

Water and Blood do not only signify Baptism and the Eucharist, but other Sacraments as well. The pale ray does not only stand for Baptism but also for Penance; whereas the red ray, apart from the Eucharist, stands also for Confirmation, the Anointing of the Sick, Holy Order and Matrimony.

Considering the above explanation, Jesus' words concerning the rays can be easily understood: "The two rays denote Blood and Water. The pale ray stands for the Water which makes souls righteous. The red ray stands for the Blood which is the life of souls."

It must be stressed once again that the rays, symbols of the value of Jesus' death play a very special role in the Devotion. They stand for Blood and Water and are therefore the subject of the Devotion. They are worshipped in a simple prayer *O Blood and Water* which Jesus taught Sister Faustina and to which He attached a promise addressed, however, only to her.

The inscription, Jesus I Trust in You

According to Jesus' will expressed in the first vision of Sister Faustina, the image should have an inscription *Jesus, I trust in You*. While the picture was being painted, Father Sopoćko suggested another inscription, namely *Christ, King of Mercy*. Our Saviour, however, wanted the words *Jesus, I trust in You*, although He did not insist on them. The words are not as important as the meaning they convey - the idea of trustfulness and total dependence. Therefore, the inscription might consist of different words, e.g. *Jesus, I depend on You*, or *Jesus, I totally rely on You*.

The inscription *Jesus, I trust in You* is a source of comfort, hope and peace for all suffering and tormented souls. On the one hand, it strongly emphasises the necessity of trustfulness associated with practising the Devotion and on the other, reminds us of the trust Jesus places in us and the mercy we show to others.

In the vision of 1934, Jesus described His gaze in the image as His *gaze from the cross*. Rev Sopoćko, who played an important part in painting the first picture interpreted it literally, i.e. as a gaze directed *downwards*. Jesus indeed looks down in the first picture ever made,

The Divine Mercy,
painted by Stanislaw Kaczor Batowski in 1943, Cracow.

and in the others which originated under influence of Father Sopoćko. Another interpretation of the *gaze from the cross* was given by Father Józef Andrasz SJ, Sister Faustina's second spiritual director. According to him, these words should be understood as a gaze full of mercy for all the people who were redeemed by Jesus' death on the cross. This interpretation was the basis of the painting made by Adolf Hyla from Cracow which raised strong objections from Rev Sopoćko.

The promises

Jesus attached some promises to the worship of the image. A general promise given in the vision of 1934 said: "I am offering people a vessel with which they are to keep coming for graces to the fountain of mercy." Thus Jesus did not limit the number or the range of the graces. He is ready to bestow graces through His image both now and in the life after death. There is one condition attached, however - the basic one of the whole Devotion - boundless trustfulness and deeds of mercy must accompany any requests.

Apart from the general promise, three specific promises were given as well. They were mentioned during the first vision in Plock in 1931. The first of them refers to salvation: "I promise that the soul that will venerate this image will not perish," the second one concerning progress on the way to sainthood: "I also promise victory over enemies already here on earth" ('Enemies' meaning enemies of the soul, i.e. sin and temptation) and the third one promises a happy death: "I Myself will defend it as My own glory."

The Feast of Mercy

The Feast of Mercy ranks highest among all the forms of the devotion to the Divine Mercy. It is not due to the number of visions when it was mentioned (twenty-three) but to the greatness of the promises attached to it.

During the first vision in Plock Jesus addressed Sister Faustina expressing His great desire for the Feast of Mercy to be celebrated on the first Sunday after Easter (Low Sunday). He wanted the image to be blessed on that day and priests to proclaim Divine Mercy, particularly for all sinners.

Jesus wished the Feast of Mercy to be celebrated on the first Sunday after Easter, i.e. Low Sunday. The choice of this particular Sunday is of great theological significance. The mystery of the Divine Mercy is reflected in the suffering and death of Jesus; therefore it is closely connected with the mystery of Redemption. Sister Faustina noticed that too when describing the public veneration of the image at *Ostra Brama* in Vilnius she wrote: "I see now that the work of Redemption is bound up with the work of mercy requested by the Lord." The most suitable day for the Feast of Mercy is the first Sunday after Easter since the dominant theological features of the Triduum Sacrum and the Easter Octave refer to the suffering, death and resurrection of Christ and also because the main idea in the liturgy of that day, both in prayers and in the Scripture, is the worship of God in His endless mercy.

Since the mystery of Redemption is still being realised in the Sacraments of Baptism and Penance, it should be emphasised, as Rev Sopoćko pointed out, that the Feast of Mercy ought to be connected with "the remembrance of the institution of the two Sacraments."

Low Sunday, also called *White Sunday (Dominica in Albis)* refers to the solemn ending of the Baptism of the catechumens, who after the day of Baptism - on Easter Eve - and dressed in white, used to come to church every day for a week. The first Sunday after Easter was the last time they came accompanied by their families and friends. Thus institution of the Feast of Mercy on this particular Sunday, is a visible sign of the greatness of the Divine Mercy shown to people in the Sacrament of Baptism. Taking into consideration the promises of the graces to be received during the Feast of Mercy, connection between the Sacrament of Baptism and the Sunday of the Divine Mercy seems justifiable and most appropriate.

The Sacrament of Penance

Another feature of the Feast is its link with the Sacrament of Penance which was established on Resurrection Day.

Since the theological subjects of Easter are different, the Gospel concerning the Sacrament of Penance is read on Low Sunday. Thus the celebration of the Feast of Mercy on this very Sunday puts stress on the Divine Mercy bestowed on people in the Sacrament of Penance. Another link may be observed in the worship of the image of the Divine Mercy which, as has already been mentioned, shows Christ at the moment of establishing the Sacrament of Penance.

The Feast of the Divine Mercy, according to Sister Faustina, should be preceded by a novena made on nine consecutive days starting on Good Friday. Jesus told Sister Faustina on two occasions to prepare for the feast by praying for nine days. Sister Faustina conveyed Jesus' message which was addressed to all the faithful: "By this novena, I will grant every possible grace to souls!"

The Novena

In *The Diary* a beautiful novena can be found dictated to Sister Faustina, partly by Jesus Himself, and written down by her during her first stay in hospital in Pradnik. The novena was given to Sister Faustina, and Jesus' promise was addressed only to her: "I will deny nothing to any soul whom you will bring to the fount of My mercy." So this novena, as well as the litany to the Divine Mercy is not a form of the Devotion, since no promises addressed to the faithful were attached to it. Thus both Rev Sopoćko and Rev Andrasz were mistaken when they maintained that the novena from *The Diary* was one of the forms of the Devotion. Although no promises were attached to the novena, Jesus surely wanted all the faithful who pray with the words of the novena, to get some spiritual benefit. If deep trustfulness and works of mercy accompany the novena it can be regarded as practising the Devotion, so all the promises connected with trustfulness, which is the Devotion itself, can be attributed to this prayer.

It must be stressed that, according to Sister Faustina, Jesus wanted the Feast of Mercy to be preceded by a novena consisting of the Chaplet of the Divine Mercy. Some specific promises were attached to this Chaplet. The novena may be made at any time, but the most suitable time is the period between Good Friday and Low Sunday. If it arises from trustfulness accompanied by works of mercy, it constitutes a genuine act of the Devotion.

There are no details concerning the celebration of the Feast in *The Diary*. Only three elements can be distinguished. Firstly, the Feast, according to Jesus, should be celebrated in a solemn way as a *solemnitas* of the Church; secondly, the image of the Divine Mercy ought to be venerated on that day, and thirdly, priests should preach about His *great and unfathomable mercy*. Sermons preached on that day should show the Divine Mercy as part of the work of Redemption, particularly in Christ's Passion, and aim at arousing or enlivening the attitude of trustfulness. Unfortunately, on the basis of *The Diary* it is impossible to say exactly what the veneration of the image should be. It can, however, be said that Low Sunday is the most suitable and appropriate day to bless the image in the church, as Jesus mentioned to Sister Faustina many times.

The greatness of the Feast of Mercy can be measured by the greatness of the promises which Jesus attached to it. The Saviour wants to be extremely generous on that day, and grants many exceptional graces to the faithful. In the vision of late spring 1934, he promised: "Whoever approaches the Fount of Life on this day will be granted complete remission of sins and punishment." The same promise referring to the Feast of Mercy was repeated in September 1936: "The soul that will go to Confession and receive Holy Communion shall obtain complete forgiveness of sins and punishment." A very similar promise was expressed once again during the vision of April 1937: "I want to grant a plenary indulgence to the souls that will go to Confession and receive Holy Communion on the Feast of My Mercy."

Forgiveness of sins on the Feast of Mercy

Therefore the most important grace attached to the Feast is the promise of complete forgiveness of sins and punishment, directed at all who confess their sins and receive Holy Communion on that day (a process analogous to that of the Jewish *Yom Kippur* described in the Old Testament, when people used to wash away their sins). After the author of *Iudicium alterius* it must be pointed out that such grace is theologically possible since neither it nor its conditions are contrary to the learning based on the Revelation. For practical reasons, confession may take place before the Feast, as Jesus wanted the greatest possible number of people to take advantage of the graces attached to the Feast. But the Holy Communion must be received on this day in the spirit of trustfulness indispensable for the Devotion. On the other hand, works of mercy are not indispensable since, as has been explained earlier, celebration of the Feast is a simple act of the devotion to the Divine Mercy.

According to the eminent dogmatists, the grace of complete remission of sins and punishment may be theologically compared to the sacramental grace of Baptism. That is why it is sometimes called a *second* or *new Baptism*. The greatness of this promise may seem shocking; however it does not oppose the Church's teaching in any way. What is more, the promise subjects the acquisition of graces to the condition of sacramental life, thus being an effective stimulus to receive the Holy Sacraments.

Jesus did not limit His generosity on the Feast of Mercy to one grace only: "On that day the very depths of My tender mercy are open. I pour out a whole ocean of graces upon those souls who approach the fount of My mercy

[...]. On that day are open all the divine floodgates through which graces flow." Therefore on this day, Jesus wants to bestow graces, both temporal and redemptive on everyone who asks for them with trust, but particularly on sinners.

The incomparable greatness of the graces attached to the Feast is manifested in three ways. Firstly, they are of a universal nature: all people, including those who have not practised the Devotion previously and sinners converted on this day may partake of the graces. Secondly, graces are both temporal and redemptive. And thirdly, all the graces are available on this day, provided they are asked for in spirit of trustfulness. No other form of the Devotion is connected with so many extraordinary graces.

THE CHAPLET OF THE DIVINE MERCY

Jesus taught this chaplet to Sister Faustina in Vilnius in September 1935. On Friday evening, 13th September when she was in her cell, she saw an Angel with a gloriously bright face, dressed in a dazzling robe, and who was to punish the earth as the executor of divine wrath. Sister Faustina tried to stop him, but her prayer was useless. However, when she saw the Holy Trinity and felt in her soul the power of Jesus' grace, she started praying again with inner power hitherto never experienced. When she was praying thus, in the words that she heard from within, the Angel became helpless and could not carry out the punishment.

The next morning she heard Jesus' order to pray every time she entered the chapel, in the words she had been taught the day before. As soon as she had fulfilled this wish, she heard Jesus say that this prayer served to appease His wrath.

The structure of the chaplet leaves no place for doubt. According to the vision of 14th September 1935, it begins with the *Our Father*, then the *Hail Mary* and *I believe*. On the large beads the following words should be said: 'Eternal Father, I offer You the Body and Blood, Soul and Divinity of Your dearly beloved Son, Our Lord Jesus Christ, in atonement for our sins and those of the whole world.' On the small beads one should say: 'For the sake of His sorrowful Passion have mercy on us and on the whole world.' In conclusion, one should say three times: 'Holy God, Holy Mighty One, Holy Immortal One, have mercy on us and on the whole world.' The chaplet should be said on the beads of the rosary consisting of five decades. Big rosaries consisting of fifteen decades are rarely used and only in some monasteries and convents, so they cannot be taken into consideration, nor can the smaller rosaries consisting of ten beads only - Jesus mentioned large beads and not just one bead on which to say *Eternal Father*. Only the ending of the chaplet is controversial. Its similarity to the Rosary would suggest that the prayer *Holy God, Holy Mighty One* should be said after every ten beads. This was the version favoured in the beginning by the Censor of Sister Faustina's writings in the theological analysis of the Chaplet. It seems, however, that the generally accepted custom of saying these words at the very end is more justified and consistent with the vision, although the vision itself, did not place these words in the Chaplet in a precise way.

The offering of Jesus is a voluntary act of unity with His sacrifice on the cross offered for our salvation. He made a sacrifice for us, so in a sense belongs to us and may be offered by us to the Eternal Father. In this act we are united to Jesus' sacrifice on the cross and appeal to God's love for all people which was most profoundly expressed in our Saviour's Passion. Similarly, the words

For the sake of His sorrowful Passion refer not so much to the atonement Christ accomplished for us on the cross, as to His Father's mercy for us. Appealing to the love which was shown in Jesus' Passion, we resort to the strongest argument we can, for God to hear our prayer.

The recitation of the Chaplet, although said individually, should always be in the plural - *have mercy on us* and not *have mercy on me*. Changing plural into singular, would be against Jesus' will, because the use of the plural in the Chaplet reflects Jesus' teaching in the Our Father. When we say the Chaplet, we ask God to 'Have mercy on us and on the whole world' thus fulfilling the condition necessary to receive the Divine Mercy. *Us* means both the people saying the prayer and those they are praying for; whereas *the whole world* means all the people on earth as well as the souls in purgatory. The words 'have mercy on us and on the whole world' has yet another significance. They teach us to get rid of our egoism and put the common welfare - that of our family, friends, nation, Church, etc. before our own. The better we can do this, the better we practise the mercy demanded by God in the Devotion. Whoever said the Chaplet, thinking only of his own good would not practise the Devotion properly, and therefore would not get any graces attached to it.

While saying the Chaplet, it is necessary to be faithful to the text, which cannot be changed for any reason whatsoever. There have been a few attempts at such changes, e.g. the work '*Verehrung der göttlichen Barmherzigkeit*' published in 1993 contains the Chaplet to the Divine Mercy in which the Eternal Father is not only offered the Body and Blood, Soul and *Divinity* of Jesus Christ but also the *tears and bitterness of His Holy Mother*. While begging for the Divine Mercy, we refer not only to Jesus' sorrowful Passion but also to His Mother's suffering. Although these words surely originated from fervent devotion to Our Lady, they cannot be included in the Chaplet whose words were dictated by Jesus himself. Therefore changing the words of the Chaplet would result in giving up the rights to the graces attached to it.

Perseverance

Another important point concerning the recitation of the Chaplet is perseverance. Although Jesus promised the grace of a happy death even after a single recitation of the Chaplet, nowhere else is it said that other graces will be given immediately. It was confirmed by the vision of 22nd March 1937, when Faustina, having recited the Chaplet at the deathbed of a young man, and watching his protracted agony, wanted to start other prayers. Jesus, however, told her to repeat the Chaplet. Another proof took place on 22nd May 1937, when Sister Faustina begging for rain, recited the Chaplet for three hours. This resulted in a heavy rainfall. And the Lord let her know, that "everything can be obtained by means of this prayer." It must be emphasised that we should pray persistently, believing in the prayer's efficaciousness.

Jesus attached one general and four specific promises to the recitation of the Chaplet. The general promise was expressed in the vision of 22nd May 1937, and repeated on 28th January 1938: "It pleases Me to grant everything they ask of Me by saying the chaplet." In May 1938 Jesus added that everything could be obtained by means of this chaplet, if it is not against His will. Jesus is ready to give *everything* which means both temporal and redemptive graces for individuals as well as for communities. Similar general promises were made earlier in November and December 1936: "The souls that will say this chaplet, will be embraced by My mercy during their lifetime; Oh, what great graces I will grant to souls who say this chaplet; the very depths of My tender mercy are stirred for the sake of those who say the chaplet." Obviously, the promise is valid only if the other basic conditions of the Devotion are met, i.e. trust, perseverance and works of mercy.

The First Promise

The extraordinary and exceptional character of the promised graces is evident in the four specific promises. The first one was included in the vision of September 1936: "Whoever will recite it, will receive great mercy at the hour of death [...]. Even if there were a sinner most hardened, if he were to recite this chaplet only once, he would receive grace from My infinite mercy." This great promise refers to conversion and death in the state of grace and has nothing to do with magic, as there is a condition of trust attached to it - Jesus wants to bestow these exceptional graces on people who trust in His mercy. Therefore the promise of a happy death is valid, only when the chaplet is said in the spirit of trust and humility and results from trust in the Divine Mercy.

The Second Promise

The second specific promise of conversion and a happy death was given on 12th December 1936, to the dying, at whose deathbed other people say the chaplet: "When this chaplet is said at the bedside of a dying person, God's anger is placated, and unfathomable mercy envelops the soul, and the very depths of My tender mercy will be moved."

The Third Promise

The two promises mentioned above, refer to the eternal outcome of death, whereas the next two concern its temporal aspect. In the third promise of 28th January 1938, Jesus said: "When hardened sinners say it, I will fill their souls with peace, and the hour of their death will be a happy one." This promise was explained in the first part of the vision: "All those souls who will glorify My mercy [...] will not experience terror at the hour of death. My mercy will shield them in that final battle." This promise was directed at all the people who spread the worship of the Divine Mercy and recite the chaplet. It shows three aspects of the grace bestowed on the dying - fearlessness, peacefulness and a happy death. It must be added, that the promise is valid only when the recitation of the chaplet results from inner trustfulness in the Divine Mercy. Jesus' words of January 1938 confirm this: "Whoever places his trust in My mercy will be filled with My divine peace at the hour of death."

The Fourth Promise

The fourth promise gives the same graces to the dying, at whose deathbed the chaplet is recited: "When they say this chaplet, in the presence of the dying, I will stand between My Father and the dying person, not as the just Judge but as a merciful Saviour."

Jesus emphasises a need for trustfulness as a means of access to His Mercy, therefore graces may only be granted if the recitation of the chaplet is accompanied by the spirit of trustfulness.

The Hour of Mercy

Among numerous visions concerning the Devotion, only two refer to its next form - the hour of mercy.

The first one took place in Cracow in October 1937. Jesus instructed Faustina to observe the hour of His death - three o'clock - by thinking about His Passion and abandonment at the hour of death, and by praying for the Divine Mercy, particularly for sinners. According to our Saviour, three o'clock in the afternoon is the hour of great mercy when His generosity is endless.

Four months later, He reminded Sister Faustina that at three o'clock she should worship the Divine Mercy interceding for the whole world, and particularly for sinners. He stressed once again, that this is the hour of great mercy when anything could be granted. Jesus gave His *Secretary* detailed advice on how to pray at the hour of mercy: making the Stations of the Cross or, in case that was not possible, a short adoration of the Blessed Sacrament in the chapel or, if that also was difficult to perform, just a short immersion in prayer wherever one happens to be.

The hour of Jesus' death was a time of great mercy for the world, and now, according to His will, it is again to be a time of great mercy for the whole world, when the Saviour will not refuse anything He is asked for. This mercy will be shown not only on Fridays but on every day at three pm There are three conditions: firstly - the prayers are to be addressed to Jesus, secondly - they have to be said at three o'clock in the afternoon, thirdly - they ought to refer to the values and merits of Jesus' Passion. Obviously, three other basic conditions must be met as well: the object of the prayer has to be in accordance with the Divine Will, it must be said in the spirit of trustfulness and it should be combined with the practice of active love of one's neighbour.

Although the second vision was addressed to Sister Faustina, its suggestions, as well as those of the first one were directed at all people. Jesus making three pm a time, particularly privileged in the Devotion, wanted us to pray then for mercy for the whole world, and especially for sinners. He instructed us to meditate on His Passion and particularly on the fact that at the moment of death He was forsaken; to those who do this, He promised the grace of understanding the value and meaning of His Passion. He also wanted us to make the Way of the Cross and, if that was not possible, to pray in front of the Blessed Sacrament adoring His Heart, or just to pray anywhere we happened to be at the time.

On the basis of the visions on Good Fridays in 1935 and 1936 it may be presumed that Jesus also wanted the image of the Divine Mercy to be adored at the hour of His death. Both visions took place at the hour of mercy, and were connected with His Passion, so Jesus' words: "I desire that the image be publicly honoured" support this opinion. Therefore the celebration of the hour of mercy may combine a few forms of the Devotion - a prayer at three o'clock, the chaplet and adoration of the image of the Divine Mercy.

The Propagation of the Worship of Mercy

The last form of the Devotion handed down by Sister Faustina was the propagation of the worship of Mercy. In *The Diary* there are five visions addressed, not only to her, but to all the worshippers. In the works of Sister Faustina there are descriptions of many visions connected with the propagation of the worship of Mercy but most of them referred only to her.

In February 1935, Jesus promised Faustina that, at the hour of death, He would protect everyone who had worshipped His great mercy. Soon after that, during adoration, Jesus promised again, to show His mercy at the time of death, to people who would propagate the Devotion.

On *Low Sunday*, 4th April 1937, Jesus said, that people who would propagate the worship of mercy would enjoy His *maternal* protection during their lives, and at the hour of death, would experience the Saviour's infinite mercy.

At the end of January 1938, Jesus addressed a special promise to priests, and propagators of the Devotion. He promised to give them *wondrous power* and inspiration, so that on hearing them speak about this unfathomable Mercy, even hardened sinners would repent.

The last vision directed at all propagators of the Divine Mercy took place on 28th January 1938. It was then that Jesus said: "All those souls who will glorify My mercy and spread its worship, encouraging others to trust in My mercy, will not experience terror at the hour of death. My mercy will shield them in that final battle."

Jesus gave no specific instructions on how the worship of mercy was to be spread, so it may be interpreted in many ways. However, to understand it as solely *giving witness with one's life in the spirit of trust in God and mercy towards one's neighbour* would be incomplete. Jesus demands *encouraging others to trust* in His mercy. Therefore, evoking trust in others is the main task of the propagators of the Divine Mercy. Trust is the essence of the Devotion, so by encouraging others to be trustful, we spread the Devotion. Thus it may be assumed that the promises addressed to the propagators of the Devotion, refer also to the propagators of its particular forms, i.e. the chaplet, the image or the Feast of Mercy.

According to Sister Faustina, there are two promises addressed to the propagators of the worship of Mercy. The first one concerns Jesus' tender protection and care throughout their lives. Although the exact meaning of this promise is not completely clear, it may be understood as extraordinary protection throughout one's life on earth. The other promise refers to the hour of death, ensuring Jesus' extraordinary mercy, similar to the one attached to the chaplet but in a higher degree, since the propagation of the worship of Mercy is more important than its adoration.

According to the promise addressed to priests, their sermons would exercise extraordinary power making sinners convert, when they spoke about the mercy and compassion of Jesus and the pity He feels for them. This *wondrous power*, inspiring words of healing and reconciliation which *touch the hearts of the listeners* should lead to conversion. One of the ways it may be realised, is in the Sacrament of Penance. Therefore, priests should preach about the Divine Mercy during retreats, missions and services preparing for confession.

It seems, however, that Jesus attached a great deal of importance to sermons preached on the Feast of Mercy. They should lead to the conversion of sinners by proclaiming the worship, adoration and praise of the Divine Mercy which was best expressed in the mystery of Redemption.

Conclusion

Jesus' message to humanity acquired a new importance when Sister Faustina was canonised on 30th April 2000, on the Feast of Mercy. At the beginning of the third millennium, it appeals to us with renewed strength. Pope John Paul II expressed this fact in his encyclical *Dives in misericordia* some years ago, and again during his visit to the shrine of the Divine Mercy in Lagiewniki, Cracow. It was during this visit that he said: "The Church renews the proclamation of the Divine Mercy to bring the light of hope to the present and future generations [...]. And this proclamation is easy enough for everybody to understand."

Indeed, the message about the Divine Mercy, given to us by Jesus, Himself, and handed down to us by Sister Faustina, is becoming more and more widely known, and is now practised in every country in the world.

THE DEVOTIONS AND PRAYERS

THE CHAPLET

The Chaplet of The Divine Mercy is said on ordinary rosary beads. It is prayed in the following order.

The Our Father,
Hail Mary,
Apostle's Creed.

On large bead before each decade

Eternal Father, I offer you the Body and Blood, Soul and Divinity of Your dearly beloved Son, Our Lord Jesus Christ, in atonement for our sins and those of the world.

Once on each of the ten small beads

For the sake of His sorrowful Passion, have mercy on us and on the whole world.

Concluding doxology

(after five decades repeat three times)
Holy God, Holy Mighty One, Holy Immortal One, have mercy on us and the whole world.

The Prayer "O Blood and Water"

"O Blood and Water, which gushed forth from the heart of Jesus as a Fount of Mercy for us, I trust in you".

NOVENA

The Novena begins on Good Friday and ends on Mercy Sunday, the first Sunday after Easter.

Novena - First Day

Today, bring to Me all mankind, especially all sinners, and immerse them in the ocean of My mercy. In this way you will console Me in the bitter grief into which the loss of souls plunges Me.

Most Merciful Jesus, whose very nature it is to have compassion on us and to forgive us, do not look upon our sins, but upon the trust which we place in Your infinite goodness. Receive us all into the abode of Your Most Compassionate Heart, and never let us escape from it. We beg this of You by Your love which unites You to the Father and the Holy Spirit.

Eternal Father, turn Your merciful gaze upon all mankind and especially upon poor sinners, all enfolded in the most Compassionate Heart of Jesus. For the sake of His sorrowful Passion, show us Your mercy, that we may praise the omnipotence of Your mercy forever and ever. Amen. *Recite the Chaplet.*

Second Day

Today bring to Me the souls of priests and religious, and immerse them in My unfathomable mercy. It was they who gave Me the strength to endure My bitter Passion. Through them, as through channels, My mercy flows out upon mankind.

Most Merciful Jesus, from whom comes all that is good, increase Your grace in us, that we may perform worthy works of mercy, and that all who see us may glorify the Father of Mercy who is in heaven.

The fountain of God's love dwells in pure hearts, bathed in the Sea of Mercy, radiant as stars, bright as the dawn. Eternal Father, turn Your merciful gaze upon the company of chosen ones in Your vineyard upon the souls of priests and religious; and endow them with the strength of Your blessing. For the love of the Heart of Your Son, in which they are enfolded, impart to them Your power and light, that they may be able to guide others in the way of salvation, and with one voice sing praise to Your boundless mercy for ages without end. Amen. *Recite The Chaplet.*

Third Day

Today bring to Me all devout and faithful souls, and immerse them in the ocean of My mercy. These souls brought Me consolation on the Way of the Cross. They were that drop of consolation in the midst of an ocean of bitterness.

Most Merciful Jesus, from the treasury of Your mercy, You impart Your graces in great abundance to each and all. Receive us into the abode of Your Most Compassionate Heart and never let us escape from it. We beg this of You by that most wondrous love for the heavenly Father with which Your Heart burns so fiercely. The miracles of mercy are impenetrable. Neither the sinner nor just one will fathom them.

When You cast upon us an eye of pity, You draw us all closer to Your love. Eternal Father, turn Your merciful gaze upon faithful souls, as upon the inheritance of Your Son. For the sake of His sorrowful Passion, grant them Your blessing and surround them with Your constant protection. Thus may they never fail in love or lose the treasure of the holy faith, but rather, with all the hosts of Angels and Saints, may they glorify Your boundless mercy for endless ages. Amen. *Recite The Chaplet.*

Fourth Day

Today bring to Me the pagans and those who do not yet know me. I was thinking also of them during My bitter Passion, and their future zeal comforted My Heart. Immerse them in the ocean of My mercy. Most Compassionate Jesus, You are the Light of the whole world.

Receive into the abode of Your Most Compassionate Heart the souls of pagans who as yet do not know You. Let the rays of Your grace enlighten them that they, too, together with us, may extol Your wonderful mercy; and do not let them escape from the abode which is Your Most Compassionate Heart.

May the light of Your love enlighten the souls in darkness; grant that these souls will know You and, together with us, praise Your mercy. Eternal Father, turn Your merciful gaze upon the souls of pagans and of those who as yet do not know You, but who are enclosed in the Most Compassionate Heart of Jesus. Draw them to the light of the Gospel. These souls do not know what great happiness it is to love You. Grant that they, too, may extol the generosity of Your mercy for endless ages. Amen. *Recite The Chaplet.*

Fifth Day

Today bring to Me the souls of heretics and schismatics, and immerse them in the ocean of My mercy. During My bitter Passion they tore at My Body and Heart; that is, My Church. As they return to unity with the Church, My wounds heal, and in this way they alleviate My Passion.

Most Merciful Jesus, Goodness Itself, You do not refuse light to those who seek it of You. Receive into the abode of Your Most Compassionate Heart the souls of heretics and schismatics. Draw them by Your light into the unity of the Church, and do not let them escape from the abode of Your Most Compassionate Heart; but bring it about that they, too, come to adore the generosity of

Your mercy. Even for those who have torn the garment of Your unity, A fount of mercy flows from Your Heart. The omnipotence of Your mercy, O God, Can lead these souls also out of error.

Eternal Father, turn Your merciful gaze upon the souls of heretics and schismatics, who have squandered Your blessings and misused Your graces by obstinately persisting in their errors. Do not look upon their errors, but upon the love of Your own Son and upon His bitter Passion, which He underwent for their sake, since they, too, are enclosed in the Most Compassionate Heart of Jesus. Bring it about that they also may glorify Your great mercy for endless ages. Amen. *Recite The Chaplet.*

Sixth Day

Today bring to Me the meek and humble souls and the souls of little children, and immerse them in My mercy. These souls most closely resemble My Heart. They strengthened Me during My bitter agony. I saw them as earthly Angels, who would keep vigil at My altars. I pour out upon them whole torrents of grace. Only the humble soul is able to receive My grace. I favour humble souls with My confidence.

Most Merciful Jesus, You yourself have said, "Learn from Me for I am meek and humble of heart." Receive into the abode of Your Most Compassionate Heart all meek and humble souls and the souls of little children.

These souls send all heaven into ecstasy, and they are the heavenly Father's favour. They are a sweet-smelling bouquet before the throne of God; God himself takes delight in their fragrance. These souls have a permanent abode in Your Most Compassionate Heart, O Jesus, and they unceasingly sing out a hymn of love and mercy. A truly gentle and humble soul already here on earth the air of paradise breathes, and in the fragrance of her humble heart the Creator Himself delights.

Eternal Father, turn Your merciful gaze upon meek and humble souls, and upon the souls of little children, who are enfolded in the abode which is the Most Compassionate Heart of Jesus. These souls bear the closest resemblance to Your Son. Their fragrance rises from the earth and reaches Your very throne. Father of mercy and of all goodness, I beg You by the love You bear these souls and by the delight You take in them: bless the whole world, that all souls together may sing out the praises of Your mercy for endless ages. Amen. *Recite The Chaplet.*

Seventh Day

Today bring to Me the souls who especially venerate and glorify My mercy, and immerse them in My mercy. These souls sorrowed most over My Passion and entered most deeply into My Spirit. They are living images of My Compassionate Heart. These souls will shine with a special brightness in the next life. Not one of them will go into the fire of hell. I shall particularly defend each one of them at the hour of death.

Most Merciful Jesus, whose Heart is Love Itself, receive into the abode of Your Most Compassionate Heart the souls of those who particularly extol and venerate the greatness of Your mercy. These souls are mighty with the very power of God Himself. In the midst of all afflictions and adversities they go forward, confident of Your mercy. These souls are united to Jesus and carry all mankind on their shoulders. These souls will not be judged severely, but Your mercy will embrace them as they depart from this life. A soul who praises the goodness of her Lord, she is always close to the living fountain and draws graces from Mercy Divine.

Eternal Father, turn Your merciful gaze upon the souls who glorify and venerate Your greatest attribute, that of Your fathomless mercy, and who are enclosed in the Most Compassionate Heart of Jesus. These souls are a living Gospel; their hands are full of deeds of mercy, and their spirit, overflowing with joy, sings a canticle of mercy to You, O Most High! I beg You O God: Show them Your mercy according to the hope and trust they have placed in You. Let there be accomplished in them the promise of Jesus, who said to them, I Myself will defend as My own glory, during their lifetime, and especially at the hour of their death, those souls who will venerate My fathomless mercy. Amen. *Recite The Chaplet.*

Eighth Day

Today bring to Me the souls who are in the prison of Purgatory, and immerse them in the abyss of My mercy. Let the torrents of My Blood cool down their scorching flames. All these souls are greatly loved by Me. They are making retribution to My justice. It is in your power to bring them relief. Draw all the indulgences from the treasury of My Church and offer them on their behalf. Oh, if you only knew the torments they suffer, you would continually offer for them the alms of the spirit and pay off their debt to My justice.

Most Merciful Jesus, You Yourself have said that You desire mercy; so I bring into the abode of Your Most Compassionate Heart the souls in Purgatory, souls who are very dear to You, and yet, who must make retribution to Your justice. May the streams of Blood and Water which gushed forth from Your Heart put out the flames of the purifying fire, that in that place, too, the power of Your mercy may be praised. From the terrible heat of the cleansing fire rises a plaint to Your mercy, and they receive comfort, refreshment, relief in the stream of mingled Blood and Water.

Eternal Father, turn Your merciful gaze upon the souls suffering in Purgatory, who are enfolded in the Most Compassionate Heart of Jesus. I beg You, by the sorrowful Passion of Jesus Your Son, and by all the bitterness with which His most sacred soul was flooded, manifest Your mercy to the souls who are under Your just scrutiny. Look upon them in no other way than through the Wounds of Jesus, Your dearly beloved Son; for we firmly believe that there is no limit to Your goodness and compassion. Amen. *Recite The Chaplet.*

Ninth Day

Today bring to Me souls who have become lukewarm, and immerse them in the abyss of My mercy. These souls wound My Heart most painfully.

My soul suffered the most dreadful loathing in the Garden of Olives because of lukewarm souls. They were the reason I cried out: "Father, take this cup away from Me, if it be Your will." For them, the last hope of salvation is to flee to My mercy.

Most compassionate Jesus, You are Compassion Itself. I bring lukewarm souls into the abode of Your Most Compassionate Heart. In this fire of Your pure love let these tepid souls, who, like corpses, filled You with such deep loathing, be once again set aflame. O Most Compassionate Jesus, exercise the omnipotence of Your mercy and draw them into the very ardour of Your love; and bestow upon them the gift of holy love, for nothing is beyond Your power. Fire and ice cannot be joined; Either the fire dies, or the ice melts. But by Your mercy, O God, You can make up for all that is lacking.

Eternal Father, turn Your merciful gaze upon lukewarm souls, who are nonetheless enfolded in the Most Compassionate Heart of Jesus. Father of Mercy, I beg You by the bitter Passion of Your Son and by His three-hour agony on the Cross: Let them, too, glorify the abyss of Your mercy. Amen. *Recite The Chaplet.*

Mercy Sunday - First Sunday after Easter

The Lord wants this day reserved as "Mercy Sunday". In order to complete the Novena one must go to Confession, Mass, and Holy Communion on this first Sunday After Easter.

Ask a priest to hear your Confession before Mass and Holy Communion.

Hour of Mercy 3 pm

This may be said at the hour of Jesus' death, not only on Fridays but every day.

Pray for mercy for the whole world and especially for sinners. Appropriate Prayer:

You expired, Lord Jesus, but the source of life gushed forth for souls and the ocean of mercy opened up for the whole world. O Fount of life, unfathomable Divine Mercy, envelop the whole world and empty yourself out upon us.

The chaplet may also be recited together with worship of the image.

Sister Faustina's Litany of the Divine Mercy

Divine Mercy, gushing forth from the bosom of the Father, I Trust in You.

Divine Mercy, greatest attribute of God, I Trust in You.

Divine Mercy, incomprehensible mystery, I Trust in You.

Divine Mercy, fountain gushing forth from the mystery of the Most Blessed Trinity, I Trust in You.

Divine Mercy, unfathomed by any intellect, human or angelic, I Trust in You.

Divine Mercy, from which wells forth all life and happiness, I Trust in You.

Divine Mercy, better than the heavens, I Trust in You.

Divine Mercy, source of miracles and wonders, I Trust in You.

Divine Mercy, encompassing the whole universe, I Trust in You.

Divine Mercy, descending to earth in the Person of the Incarnate Word, I Trust in You.

Divine Mercy, which flowed out from the open wound of the Heart of Jesus, I Trust in You.

Divine Mercy, enclosed in the Heart of Jesus for us, and especially for sinners, I Trust in You.

Divine Mercy, unfathomed in the institution of the Sacred Heart, I Trust in You.

Divine Mercy, in the founding of Holy Church, I Trust in You.

Divine Mercy, in the Sacrament of Holy Baptism, I Trust in You.

Divine Mercy, in our justification through Jesus Christ, I Trust in You.

Divine Mercy, accompanying us through our whole life, I Trust in You.

Divine Mercy, embracing us especially at the hour of death, I Trust in You.

Divine Mercy, endowing us with immortal life, I Trust in You.

Divine Mercy, accompanying us every moment of our life, I Trust in You.

Divine Mercy, shielding us from the fire of hell, I Trust in You.

Divine Mercy, in the conversion of hardened sinners, I Trust in You.

Divine Mercy, astonishment for Angels, incomprehensible to Saints, I Trust in You.

Divine Mercy, unfathomed in all the mysteries of God, I Trust in You.

Divine Mercy, lifting us out of every misery, I Trust in You.

Divine Mercy, source of our happiness and joy, I Trust in You.

Divine Mercy, in calling us forth from nothingness to existence, I Trust in You.

Divine Mercy, embracing all the works of His hands, I Trust in You.

Divine Mercy, crown of all of God's handiwork, I Trust in You.

Divine Mercy, in which we are all immersed, I Trust in You.

Divine Mercy, sweet relief for anguished hearts, I Trust in You.

Divine Mercy, only hope of despairing souls, I Trust in You.

Divine Mercy, repose of hearts, peace amidst fear, I Trust in You.

Divine Mercy, delight and ecstacy of holy souls, I Trust in You.

Divine Mercy, inspiring hope against all hope, I Trust in You.

Eternal God, in whom mercy is endless and the treasury of compassion inexhaustible, look kindly upon us and increase Your mercy in us, that in difficult moments we might not despair nor become despondent, but with great confidence submit ourselves to Your holy will, which is Love and Mercy itself.

Vincent de Paul

Amid the wars and turmoil of 16th-century
Reformation France, and in the midst of great
suffering and poverty, Providence provided an
amazing example of apostolic zeal. Highly intelligent,
physically small, and burning with love for Christ in
the poor, Vincent de Paul stimulated a major change
in the social consciousness of France and far beyond.
His Religious Orders for men and women continue
today. This account of his life and times captures the
amazing spirit of this humble and courageous man,
who truly loved and served the poor.

Barry Midgley, a retired
Headmaster, has spent most of his
professional life in Catholic
education. He has published
several titles with CTS and lives in
East Anglia.

ISBN: 978 1 86082 503 3

CTS Code: B 701